Catching Brilliance

SIMPLE REFLECTIONS TO NURTURE THE SOUL

WRITTEN AND ILLUSTRATED BY
WENDY DEWAR HUGHES

 SUMMER BAY PRESS

Catching Brilliance

SIMPLE REFLECTIONS TO NURTURE THE SOUL

WRITTEN AND ILLUSTRATED BY
WENDY DEWAR HUGHES

Catching Brilliance - Simple Reflections to Nurture The Soul

Copyright 2018 © Wendy Dewar Hughes

All rights reserved. Artwork and writing is all original work of Wendy Dewar Hughes. No part of this publication may be reproduced, stored in a retrieval system, or transmitted in any form or by any means – electronic, mechanical, digital, photocopy, recording, or any other – without the prior permission of the author.

www.wendydewarhughes.com

Published by Summer Bay Press.
Agassiz, British Columbia V0M 1A2
www.summerbaypress.com

Editing, Interior Design and Cover Design:
Wendy Dewar Hughes, Summer Bay Press

ISBN: 978-1-927626-80-1
Digital ISBN: 978-1-927626-81-8

Constantly thinking about the past and the future means you won't enjoy the present while you're in it. Stay present.

You have been given the gift of creativity for a reason. That reason is simply to create.

Enjoy the process, the journey, the moment. It will not come again.

Live simply, love generously, allow yourself to care deeply.

Be kind.

Allow joy to bless you with encouragement today. Find at least one thing to be joyful about and see your day change for the better.

Immerse yourself in the life you desire. Give it all you've got.

Before you can start something new,
be sure you actually to want to.

Sometimes we set out on a path
because we believe we should,
not because we want to.

*What would you do
if fear did not exist?
Imagine your life without any fear
and see where you can go.*

Look for the joy in everything
that you do.

Your creative experience
should be a joyful one.

Where you are right now is where you should be and is a cause for celebration. Look at how far you've come, not how far you have to go.

Take courage.

Ask for what you really want.

Decide what you want to do and tell everyone. That's how connections are made with people who can help you make your dreams to come true.

Are you "under the circumstances"?
Don't let them define your life.
Get out from under them.

Your world will conform to your own expectations. Change your expectations and you will change your experience.

The common belief is that no one likes change. This isn't true. People don't want to change when they fear that the change will result in something worse. When it's obvious that change will bring improvement, it is welcomed.

Sometimes you have to let go of something in order for something new to come into your life. Think about what no longer needs to take up space in your life and remove it.

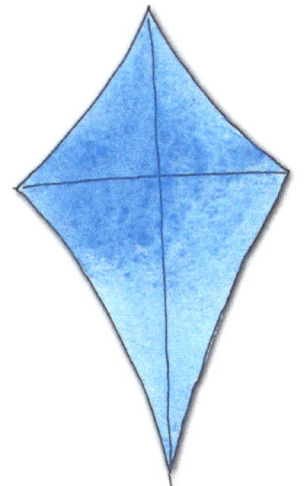

You may have to let go of doing everything yourself in order to move into a bigger realm. No one moves into big things while trying to do all the small things themselves.

Being a boss and being a leader is not the same thing. Leaders must be willing to go ahead of the crowd not just give orders from the rear.

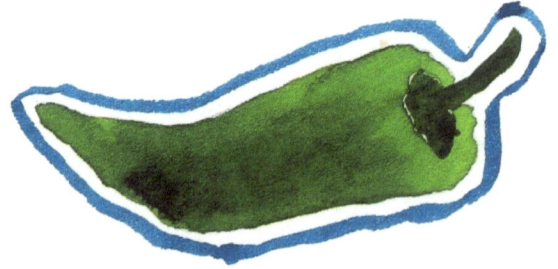

Growth takes courage and courage requires decision. Once you make the decision, courage will give you the fuel to grow.

Now is the only moment you have. The past is behind and the future does not exist. Live your best life right now.

Your pay does not determine your value, you do. Decide how to be of value and you will be paid.

Don't live in the future or the past. You can't change the past and when you get to the future it will be the present. Live in the present.

Turn your "what if" into what is by making the decision to do it. Everything is possible to the one who believes.

Ask for what you want without apology or whining. The decisive person is the determined person.

Give yourself permission to follow the call of your heart. The call of your heart is the heart of your calling.

Be willing to become outstanding in what you do.
Do not allow the opinions of others to determine your life.

Be grateful for the gift of life.
You did nothing to earn it.
Your life is a gift.

Relax and believe that right now you are in the right place at the right time.

Slow down and think. Allow yourself time to consider your life, what is important and what is not.
Life is best lived at a relaxed pace.

Buy yourself something that you have wanted for a long time.
Find the perfect one.

You are unique, one of a kind and so loved. Always remember that.

Define what success means to
you, not what society or culture
says it should be.
Listen to your own heart.
It will change everything.

Learn to appreciate silence. In quietness and confidence will be your strength.

You are worthy of knowing God personally. After all, God knows you personally.

It is always a two-way relationship.

Decide what you want and know why, then just start taking steps in the direction of your dreams.

Feeling discouraged? Take a few minutes to write a gratitude list. You'll be amazed at how changing your perspective will change your mood.

Having difficulty finishing
a project?
Try taking a break and coming
back to it with new eyes.

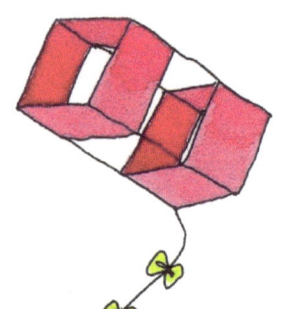

Are you more conscious of prosperity or of lack? You can tell by how much you worry about whether or not you will have enough.

Finish things. The satisfaction you'll have for completing a project will give you energy for the next one.

Allow yourself to feel totally irresponsible for five or ten minutes. Give yourself a break and be a kid.

Emotional pain can be an indication that you're not being true to yourself. Get quiet and listen to your own heart.

Remove all judgments from your creative process. Nothing you create is good or bad, it just is.

You deserve to enjoy your own life and to create what you love.
No one can dictate what is of value to you except you.

Take a day off and
do something just
for the fun of it.
Play energizes and
reminds us that life
is to be enjoyed.

Just take the next step. You don't always have to see the end from the beginning. Know where you're headed and just keep taking steps. You'll get there.

Nourish your creative side with fun.
Try seeing life as a child again and
allow your attention to wander to
whatever takes your fancy.

Rather than writing in your journal, try drawing to express what you want to say. Besides being fun, it is good brain exercise. Don't judge your sketches.

You don't always have to see the end from the beginning. Know where you're headed and just take the next step. You will get there.

Playfulness adds
balance to your life.
Let go of being an overly
responsible adult for a while.

Patience and waiting is a form of action when your mind is busy creating. Books and art are born in the mind before the hands begin to work.

Add some silliness to your daily life. Wear crazy socks, collect fun toys, play games, make jokes, make up stories and have fun.

Perfectionism will prevent you from starting anything that might make you look foolish or might not turn out well. Allow yourself to blow it now and then.

It is often easier to react than it is to stop and think. Give yourself time to really think today rather than just reacting to outside stimulus.

Remember your original vision and
why you're doing what you're doing.
Is it still important to you?

Forgive.
Let it go.
Let them off the hook.
Move on.

Trust your own intuition to know what is true for you. Always listen to your own heart.

Don't let a lack of confidence prevent you from getting started. Practice creates confidence and moves you to competence. In doing, your confidence will grow.

Expect life to be difficult and difficulty will be all you see. Believe instead that life is easy and joyful and that is what your experience will be.

Find something new to love everyday.
You'll be surprised at how doing
this will lift your mood.

The future arrives one moment at a time. When it does, you will be ready for it.

Take care of yourself without feeling selfish. You have to be prepared for whatever you need to do.

Imagine your work pleasing your audience. Whether you write or create art, envision your audience enjoying what you create.

If you want to spend more time creating, spend less time watching television or surfing the Internet. Guard your creative time.

Connect with other people who love what you love. They will understand you when others may not.

Place yourself in the presence of grandeur. Watch a sunset, visit a canyon, watch the ocean waves, or gaze at the mountains.

Nobody holds your future in his or her hands but God. You don't have to please anyone else.

Welcome the unexpected
rather than getting upset.
It may hold some wonderful
surprises for you.

Trust you own intuition.
The more you do, the more your confidence will grow.

Don't talk yourself out of wanting what you really want because you think you can't have it. Your heart knows what you need.

When you feel completely free to be yourself you inspire others to do so, too.

Ideas sometimes appear bizarre when they first appear. Before you discard them, invite them in and entertain them for a while. Sometimes the most peculiar ideas turn out to be the best ones.

If you're not having fun, it's time to re-evaluate what you're doing. Go for the joy.

Stop ignoring or tolerating your pain. Pain is a message to you; it's like a gift that requires opening and examining.

Feel your feelings and pay attention to them. You don't always have to analyze them. Just allow yourself to feel.

A lively curiosity will make your life more interesting. There will always be something new to think about.

Try doing something audacious.
See what happens.

Don't deny yourself pleasures in life because of lack of money. If you want something, believe that you will find a way.

Do you have barriers of resistance? You can tell if your first impulse to something new is to say no.

Invent new reasons to celebrate.
A celebration needn't be a party,
though it can be, but may be
something as simple as giving
yourself something sweet.

You don't have to do what everyone else does in order to be happy. You can choose to be happy regardless of what happens around you.

Imagine a life beyond your wildest dreams. If you can't, it's time to upgrade your wildest dreams.

Move beyond limitations by doing something completely different.
If you write, try painting.
If you paint, try sculpture.
If you sculpt, try music.

What did you pretend to be when you were a child? If this gives you joy, why not bring more of it into your life today?

Do you have a dream board? Creating a board with what you love or wish for will help you focus your mind on bringing those things into your life.

You can take the tiniest baby steps you need to move you toward your dreams. You get to choose what those steps are and how much time you spend on them.

Do you feel blocked in your creative projects? Pay attention to what inspires you in other pursuits and what you are passionate about.

Think about all the skills you have for which you are thankful. Sometimes we forget the wonderful abilities we already have.

Are you making your creative work a priority? Not honoring your creative cravings is not honoring your own soul.

Don't become immobilized; just direct your creative impulses toward something different for a while.

Is what you are doing moving you toward your goals? Or is it gobbling up time that could be better used creating the life you want?

OTHER BOOKS BY WENDY DEWAR HUGHES

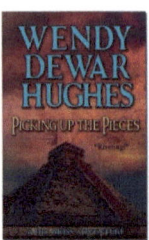
Available in Print and E-book

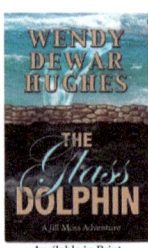
Available in Print and E-book

Available in Print and E-book

Available in E-book Only

Available in Print and E-book

Available in E-book Only

Available in Print and E-book

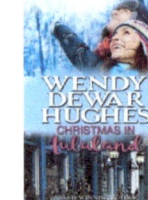
Available in Print and E-book

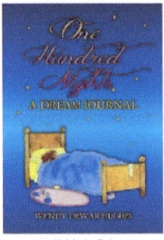
Available in Print

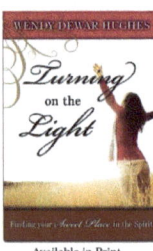
Available in Print and E-book

Available in E-book Only

Available in E-book Only

Available in Print

Available in Print

Available in Print and E-book

Available in Print

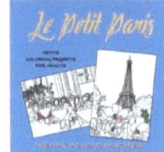
Available in Print